to:_____

from:_____

There are so many **beautiful** things I want to share with you! Let's turn the page for a **seek** and **find** **adventure** for us to do!

Can you find the pig in a party **hat?**

looky looky for the pink **pig**... can you find the one wearing a brown **wig?**

Is there a bright **yellow** sun?

looky looky for the sharks that **smile**... can you find the one with great **style?**

can you find 2 yellow stars?

ball

Where oh where is the bumble bee?

fish

looky looky for the seahorse... is there one taking math? of course!

can you spot the **raccoon** dancing under the moon?

do you see **6** pink flowers?

looky looky for the baby animals at **play**...can you find the elephant shouting **"hooray!"**?

Can you find the **pink** giraffe?

are there **5** hearts?

looky looky for the baby giraffe with its neck so **long**... can you find the one singing a song?

Can you find the **Yellow** elephant?

looky looky for the baby elephant that's **blue**... Can you find the one dancing in a **pink tutu?**

do you spot a **red** balloon?

STOP

Can you find the taxi **honk, honk, honking** his horn?

looky looky at all the **things that go…** can you find the dump truck hauling **snow?**

is there a **purple** stop sign?

Can you spot the construction worker doing a **handstand?**
do you see **5 red** hard hats?
beep beep!
is there a **zebra** driving the crane?

Can you find 4 construction **cranes?**

beep beep!

looky looky for the pickup truck honking **beep beep!** Can you find the one being driven by a **sheep?**

Can you find the **lion** flying a plane?

howdy!

looky looky for the **plane**... Can you find the one flying through **rain?**

Before our adventure comes to an end, there's one last thing that needs a look... Can you find all 23 elephants hiding in the pages of this book?

Now you see that our world is an awesome place to explore. We can go back to the beginning and seek and find some more!

Big heartfelt thanks to Karen Botti and Hannah
Magsamen Barry. Their creativity and generous
spirits are unique and valued gifts to me and
the work we create in the studio.

Published by Sourcebooks Wonderland, an imprint of Sourcebooks Kids
P.O. Box 4410, Naperville, Illinois 60567-4410
(630) 961-3900
sourcebookskids.com

Library of Congress Cataloging-in-Publication
Data is on file with the publisher.

Source of Production:
Wing King Tong,
Shenzhen, Guangdong Province, China
Date of Production: April 2020
Run Number: 5018101

Printed and bound in China.
WKT 10 9 8 7 6 5 4 3 2 1